The Berkeley Square "Horror"

According to legend, anyone who spent a night in the haunted room at the top of No. 50 Berkeley Square would either die or go mad.

In 1887 two sailors decided to sleep in the room. In the middle of the night they heard noises. Something was crawling or creeping toward the door of the room. The candles went out. The men never did get a good look at the thing. One of the sailors tried to attack the "Horror" with a curtain rod. The other ran out the door. He found a policeman down the street and dragged him back to No. 50.

At the foot of the stairs inside they found the first sailor. He was dead. His face was frozen in an expression of terror. He had died of fright. . . .

The World's Most Famous GHOSTS

DANIEL COHEN

AN ARCHWAY PAPERBACK
Published by POCKET BOOKS • NEW YORK

Illustrations on the following pages are used by permission and through the courtesy of the Library of Congress, 4; The New York Historical Society, New York City, 39, 45, 46; New York Public Library, 6, 7, 9, 13, 14, 17, 18, 19, 21, 22, 24, 26, 27, 30, 33, 34, 41, 57, 59, 61, 65, 67, 70, 83, 85, 90, 92, 94; Robert Estall, 75, 79.

An Archway Paperback published by
POCKET BOOKS, a division of Simon & Schuster, Inc.
1230 Avenue of the Americas, New York, N.Y. 10020

Published by arrangement with Dodd, Mead & Company
Library of Congress Catalog Card Number: 77-16857

ISBN: 0-671-54630-9

First Pocket Books printing September, 1979

10 9 8 7 6 5 4

AN ARCHWAY PAPERBACK and colophon are
registered trademarks of Simon & Schuster, Inc.

Printed in the U.S.A.

IL 4+

For Herman Zeranski

CONTENTS

The World's Most Famous
GHOSTS

Introduction

A WHO'S WHO OF GHOSTS

What do Abraham Lincoln, Anne Boleyn, the voodoo queen of New Orleans, and Aaron Burr's second wife have in common? Not much, really, except that they have all been seen as ghosts.

In this book we are going to explore the tales surrounding some of the world's most famous ghosts. There are several kinds of ghost stories. There are those stories which are completely made up. Then there are those which have been investigated, and for which there is a good deal of evidence. The stories in this book fall somewhere between these two groups. They are ghostly legends.

You may believe what you like about them.

But believe them or not, I do hope you enjoy them.

People have been telling ghost stories like this for centuries. They are one of the oldest and most popular forms of entertainment in the world. If you get a bit of spooky pleasure from these tales, you are in good company.

1

LINCOLN'S GHOST

America's greatest ghost is Abraham Lincoln. The spirit of the sixteenth President has been seen in the halls of the White House. It has also been reported walking near the Lincoln grave in Springfield, Illinois. Still others say they have witnessed the dead President's ghostly funeral train.

It is no surprise that there are many Lincoln ghost stories. He was the sort of man around whom legends collect. There are so many tales about Abraham Lincoln that it is hard to separate myth from reality. But ghost stories fit him very well.

Ghosts are often said to be the spirits of peo-

Abraham Lincoln, America's most famous ghost

ple whose lives were cut short by violence. Lincoln was shot on April 14, 1865. He died the next day. That was just five days after the surrender of the South in the Civil War. His term in office still had over three years to run. There was a great deal more he could have done if he had lived.

Lincoln was also the first American President to be assassinated. Unfortunately, he was not to be the last.

Lincoln may have been interested in ghosts during his life. When he was a young lawyer in Illinois he was known as a tough-minded skeptic. But he was also said to have dabbled in spiritualism. Spiritualists believe that the living can talk with the dead. In order to communicate, a spirit "medium" is needed. A medium is a person who is supposed to have special powers. These powers are often called psychic powers. They allow the medium to see and hear things that others cannot. When a medium is around, the spirits may also do things like move tables. At least that is what spiritualists believe.

Spiritualism started in America. It was very popular in Lincoln's time. Many people went to séances. Séances are meetings held for the purpose of communicating with the dead. Even people who did not believe in spiritualism went

William Wallace Lincoln, who died in the
White House

to séances. They wanted to see what was going on.

Lincoln's wife, Mary Todd Lincoln, was also interested in spiritualism. Her interest grew after the death of her young son William. William died while the Lincolns were living in

Mary Todd Lincoln. She was interested in ghosts.

the White House. His ghost has also been reported there.

Lincoln is said to have attended several séances in the White House during his time in office. If he did, that may have been to please his wife.

At one of these séances a large piano was said to rise into the air when the medium placed her hand on it. During the darkest days of the Civil War, another medium was supposed to have come to the White House. She said she was in touch with great leaders of the past. They gave the President suggestions about the war.

Some people also believe that Lincoln himself was psychic. At times he would sit silently for hours. It was almost as if he were in a trance. There is also a story that he foresaw his own death in a dream. In fact, he had these forbidding dreams several times.

Once he reported a dream in which he saw himself inside a coffin. He was told that the President was killed by an assassin. He had this dream just ten days before he really was killed by an assassin. On the morning of his assassination he told of another warning dream. He dreamed of being on a ship bound for an unknown place.

Lincoln's bodyguard, W. H. Crook, said the

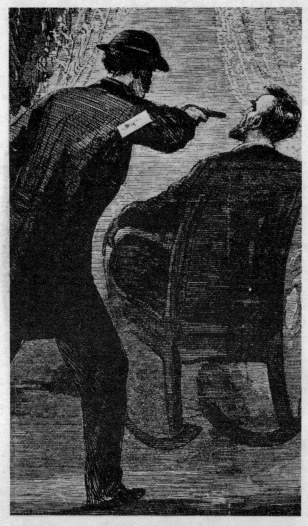

The assassination of President Lincoln

President knew he would be killed that night.
Crook said that Lincoln had warning dreams
for three nights before the assassination. The
bodyguard begged Lincoln not to go to the
theater on April 14. But Lincoln insisted, and
he was shot. The assassin was an actor names
John Wilkes Booth.

There is not necessarily anything unusual
about these stories. Lincoln was a moody man.
He was often deeply depressed. It is no surprise that he dreamed of assassination. His life
had been threatened many times. Confederates
and their sympathizers blamed Lincoln for the
loss of the war. Many of them wanted to get
even. One of them, John Wilkes Booth, did.
But all of these stories have added to the legend of Abraham Lincoln.

For many years members of the White
House staff thought they heard mysterious
footsteps on the second floor. They said the
footsteps were made by Lincoln's ghost. The
first person who actually reported seeing the
ghost was Grace Coolidge. She was the wife
of Calvin Coolidge, the thirtieth president.
Mrs. Coolidge said she saw the figure of Lincoln staring out a window of the Oval Room.

Lincoln's ghost seems to have been unusually active during the terms of President Frank-

lin D. Roosevelt. One of the guests at the Roosevelt White House was Queen Wilhelmina of the Netherlands. One night she heard a knock at her door. When she opened it she saw the tall top-hatted figure of Lincoln standing in the hall.

She reported the incident to President Roosevelt the next morning. He did not seem surprised. He said that the Queen's bedroom was known as the Lincoln Room. He then told her that the ghost had been reported by others.

One of Roosevelt's secretaries said she saw the ghost sitting on the bed in the Lincoln Room. He was pulling off his boots. That experience frightened her badly.

There is also a story that the ghost once tried to set fire to the bed in the Lincoln Room. The woman who was sleeping there immediately left the White House. Such an act seems out of character for Lincoln, alive or dead.

Relatively few people reported actually seeing the ghost. But many people in the White House said they felt its presence. President Roosevelt had a Scottish terrier named Fala. The little dog would often begin barking at something no one else could see. People said it was the ghost.

President Harry Truman was once asked about a knock he heard on his bedroom door in the White House. Truman answered, "Yes, I heard the knock and answered it about three o'clock in the morning. There wasn't anybody there. I think it must have been Lincoln's ghost walking the hall." Later Truman said he was joking about the ghost, but he did hear the knock.

Lincoln's ghost seems to have disappeared from the White House after the Truman administration. People say the reason was that many parts of the building were changed at that time. The White House had been in very poor shape. Major renovations were needed.

The ghost of Dolly Madison, wife of the fourth president, was reported to have appeared over 100 years later during the term of Woodrow Wilson. In her day Dolly Madison planted a rose garden at the White House. Mrs. Wilson wanted to have it dug up. The ghost of Dolly appeared to discourage the gardeners. The rose garden is still there.

A seamstress working in the Rose Room of the White House heard ghostly laughter and felt a strange chill. That room had once been President Andrew Jackson's bedroom. And there are many other ghostly tales attached to the White House.

But to return to Abraham Lincoln. After his

Lincoln's funeral

death, several spirit mediums reported being in communication with him. At Lincoln's grave in Springfield, Illinois, there are stories that his ghost has been seen. There are also stories that Lincoln is not really buried in the grave.

Then there is the phantom funeral train. After Lincoln was killed, his body was taken back to Illinois for burial. It was carried on a special funeral train. All along the route people lined the tracks to see the train pass.

Ever since then, according to legend, a ghostly funeral train takes the same route at the same time every year. The train is covered with black. The engine is manned by skeletons.

This description appeared in the newspaper, the *Albany Evening Times*:

"It passes noiselessly. If it is moonlight, clouds come over the moon as the phantom train goes by. After the pilot engine passes, the funeral train itself with flags and streamers rushes past. The track seems covered with black carpet, and the coffin is seen in the center of the car, while all about it in the air and on the train behind are vast numbers of blue-coated men, some with coffins on their backs, others leaning upon them."

The ghost of Abraham Lincoln and the phantom train are among America's most haunting legends.

Lincoln's funeral train

2

THE BLOODY TOWER

"There is no sadder spot on Earth."

That is what the historian Lord Macaulay said about the Tower of London. The Tower of London was first built about 900 years ago. Over the centuries many buildings have been added. Today it is a national monument in England. It is probably London's most popular tourist attraction. The Crown Jewels of Britain are on display there. But for most of its existence the Tower of London has been a fortress and a prison. It has also been a place of execution.

No one knows how many people have been executed there. Probably thousands. They have ranged from common thieves to queens

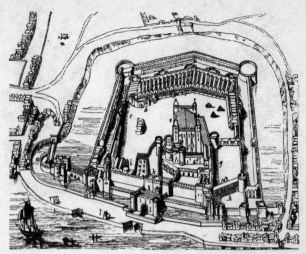

The Tower of London in 1597

The Tower of London in 1833

The place of execution in the Tower

and princes. If restless spirits haunt the place where they died, the Tower of London should be well haunted. Naturally, there are many, many ghost stories attached to the Tower of London.

Perhaps the saddest event in the Tower's long sad history was the murder of the two little princes. In 1483, twelve-year-old Edward V and his ten-year-old brother Richard, Duke of York, were imprisoned in the Tower. It was a time of great political trouble in England. The two boys were not officially executed. They were secretly murdered. Suspicion fell on their uncle, the Duke of Gloucester. With the boys out of the way he could become king. After their death he did. He took the name Richard

*The boy king,
Edward V*

*Below, King Edward V and his brother, the Duke
of York, who were murdered in the Tower.*

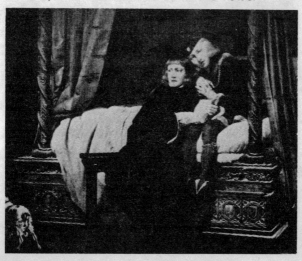

III. There is no solid proof that Richard ordered the murder. He always denied it. There were others who would have profited from the boys' deaths. But Richard III has a bad reputation. Guilty or not, he has been blamed by practically everyone.

For centuries the Tower was said to be haunted by the ghosts of the little princes. In 1674, some alterations were being made on the Tower. Workmen came upon a wooden chest containing the skeletons of two young boys. It was assumed these were the remains of the princes. The king at the time, Charles II, ordered that the skeletons be given a royal burial. Since then the boys' ghosts have not troubled the Tower.

Sir Walter Raleigh was imprisoned in the Tower for thirteen years. On some moonlit nights his ghost can be seen walking up and down along the walls near the room in which he was kept.

In 1606, Guy Fawkes tried to blow up the Parliament buildings. He and his fellow conspirators stored a great deal of gunpowder in the cellars of the buildings. Before he could carry out his plot Guy was captured and thrown into the Tower. He was executed, but first he was horribly tortured. His screams can

Richard III. The murderer?

King Henry VIII

still be heard in the Tower, according to some stories.

The most famous of the ghost stories about the Tower concerns Anne Boleyn. Anne Boleyn was King Henry VIII's second wife. He divorced his first wife to marry Anne. The divorce caused the King a great deal of trouble.

But he soon got tired of Anne. He did not want to go through another divorce. So in 1536 he had Anne imprisoned in the Tower and beheaded. Henry had four more wives. Another one, Katherine Howard, was also beheaded in the Tower in 1542.

But Anne was always the best known and most popular of Henry's six wives. She is also the most popular ghost of the Tower of London. The ghost of Anne has been reported many times, both with and without her head.

The best-documented sighting came in 1864. The Captain of the Guard was making his rounds. He found one of his men unconscious on the ground. The man's rifle, with bayonet in place, lay underneath him. When the man awakened he said he had seen the figure of a woman in white come out of a room. It was the room in which Queen Anne had spent her last night. The figure glided toward him. He called for it to stop, but it kept on coming. He stabbed at it with his bayonet, but the bayonet went right through the figure. Then the guard knew he was facing a ghost. He fainted.

The captain didn't believe the story. He thought the man had fallen asleep while on duty. The guard was court-martialed on that charge. During the trial two other guards said they had seen the whole thing. The ghost of a

Anne Boleyn, the Tower's most famous ghost

woman had come out of the room just as their
fellow guard had said. It disappeared as soon
as he had fainted. Several other guards claimed
they too had seen the phantom while they had
been on duty near the room. The court set the
prisoner free.

Shortly before Katherine Howard's execution she escaped from her cell in the Tower. She ran down a corridor looking for help. But she found none, and was returned to her cell. Her ghost has been reported seen running frantically down that corridor.

Most of the ghosts reported at the Tower of London can be connected with some person who died there. But there are two cases which do not fall into this category.

The first took place around 1800. There has always been a round-the-clock guard near the Jewel Tower, where the Crown Jewels are kept. At about midnight the guard sensed something behind him. He turned to see a huge black bear. The creature was standing on its hind legs. Its teeth were bared in a snarl. The guard struck out at it with his bayonet. But, as with the ghost of Anne Boleyn, the weapon passed right through the figure. This guard also fainted. But he was not so lucky. He was taken to the hospital where he repeated his story to several people. He never recovered from the experience. He died a few days later.

One of those who had talked to the dying guard was Edmund Swifte. Swifte was Keeper of the Crown Jewels. He held the post for twenty-eight years. During that time he heard

Katherine Howard

many strange stories, like the one about the ghostly bear. But on one Sunday evening in October, 1817, he had an experience of his own.

He was having supper with his family in a room in the Jewel Tower. The room had once been used as a prison, but many years before it had been turned into living space for people who worked in the Tower. All the doors and windows of the room were closed. Heavy curtains had been drawn over the windows. The

The Crown Jewels of England

only light in the room came from two candles on the table.

Swifte was pouring wine for his wife. She looked up and shouted. "What is that?" Swifte turned around. He never forgot what he saw. It looked like a cylinder filled with a bubbling light-blue liquid. The family watched the thing for a couple of minutes. Then it began to move. When it got behind Swifte's wife it paused. She cried out that it had tried to grab her. Swifte picked up a chair and swung at it. The chair went right through "the thing," but it retreated and disappeared. Years later Swifte said, "Even now . . . I feel the horror of that moment."

This strange thing was never seen again. Swifte had been badly frightened, but he stayed on the job. He did not retire until 1842. That was twenty-five years after the encounter.

That particular ghost, or whatever it was, has never been seen again.

3

GHOST SHIPS

Sailing has always been a dangerous profession. In the days of wooden ships men would set out on voyages that might last months or years. They never knew whether they would come back alive. Storms, pirates, and disease were just some of the dangers they faced.

It is not surprising that sailors were very superstitious. They had many tales of ghostly or haunted ships. Without a doubt the most famous is the legend of the *Flying Dutchman*.

No one seems to know how the legend began. It has probably been around in one form or other for centuries. The ancient Greeks and

An artist's version of the ghost ship, the Flying
Dutchman

Romans had tales of phantom ships. So did the ancient Chinese. All the sailors believed it was bad luck to see a phantom ship. An early written version of the *Flying Dutchman* tale appeared in a British magazine in 1821. Later it was made into a short story, a play, and a well-known opera.

In brief, the legend goes like this: A ship was making its way around the Cape of Good Hope, the southern tip of Africa. Suddenly it ran into a terrible storm. The ship was in great danger. The crew went to the Captain and begged him to find a safe harbor.

The Captain refused. Not only did he refuse but he laughed at his men's fears. He told them he was afraid of nothing on this earth or in heaven. He then shut himself up in his cabin, smoking his pipe.

The storm got worse. The ship nearly sank. But still the Captain would not yield. In fact, he became even more stubborn. He challenged the storm to sink him. At that moment a glowing Form appeared on the deck. The crew was terrified. The Captain, however, showed no respect at all.

"Captain," said the Form, "you are very stubborn."

"And you are a rascal," answered the Captain. "Who wants a peaceful passage? I don't.

I'm asking nothing from you. Clear out unless you want your brains blown out."

With that the Captain drew his pistol and fired. But the pistol exploded in his hand. Then the Form pronounced a curse on the Captain. He was doomed to sail forever, without rest. "And since it is your delight to torment sailors, you shall torment them. For you shall be the evil spirit of the sea. Your ship shall bring misfortune to all who sight it."

"Amen to that!" cried the Captain. He was not the least put down.

After that, according to the legend, anyone who sighted the phantom ship suffered for it. The *Flying Dutchman* might lead ships onto the rocks. Or the sight of her might just turn all wine on board into vinegar. Rumors that the phantom ship had been sighted were enough to terrify sailors. Oddly though, once the story became popular among landsmen, sailors refused to take it seriously anymore.

Why was the ship called the *Flying Dutchman?* We can only guess. One possible theory is about a seventeenth-century Dutch captain named Bernard Fokke. Fokke was a daring and very skillful sailor. His journeys were so quick that some thought he had supernatural aid. The rumor spread that he had made a pact with the evil spirits. When Fokke and his ship

A painting of the ghostly Flying Dutchman

The captain of the Flying Dutchman

disappeared during a voyage the rumor was strengthened.

Phantom ships were not only seen near the Cape of Good Hope. Captain Kidd's ship is said to sail around the New England coast. The old pirate is still looking for buried treasure. Another pirate ship, that of Jean Lafitte, has appeared off Galveston, Texas. That is where Lafitte's ship is supposed to have sunk in the 1820s.

In the nineteenth century an American ship named *Dash* vanished at sea. The ghost of the ship is supposed to return to port every so often. Its mission is to pick up the souls of crew members' families after they have died.

Not all legends of phantom ships are about the ocean. The Great Lakes are extremely dangerous. Storms blow up very suddenly. Sailors say that lake storms can be worse than those on the open sea. Many, many ships have been sunk in the Great Lakes. Some have completely disappeared—except for a ghost which is seen occasionally.

The best known of the phantom ships of the Great Lakes is the *Griffin*. The *Griffin* was owned by the great French explorer, Robert Cavelier de La Salle. It was built at Niagara and first set sail on August 7, 1679. It was one of the largest, if not *the* largest, ship to sail the Great Lakes up to that time. La Salle only stayed with his ship for the first leg of her maiden voyage. He was lucky.

La Salle left his ship at Green Bay. He went

by canoe down the St. Joseph River. He was looking for a river route to the Mississippi. Eventually he found one. But not on this trip.

The *Griffin* set sail from Green Bay on September 18, 1679, bound back to Niagara. She was never seen or heard from again. She simply "sailed through a crack in the ice"—or so the legend goes.

But on some nights Lakemen have reported seeing the ghostly *Griffin* looming out of the fog.

Even an empty ship can become a ghost. The Hudson's Bay Company steamship *Baychimo* was trapped in the winter ice on a voyage to Vancouver, British Columbia. It was a hard decision to abandon the ship with its cargo of valuable furs. But the Captain felt he had no choice.

Weeks later the *Baychimo* was sighted by a party of Eskimo hunters. She had broken free of the ice. The crew went out to claim her. But when they got close she vanished.

A few years later the *Baychimo* was sighted again, this time by the American ship *Northland*. As the *Northland* drew closer a dense fog engulfed both ships. When the fog lifted the *Baychimo* was gone.

Another ghostly legend of the sea is that of the *"Palatine* Light." In the winter of 1752 a Dutch ship, the *Palatine,* set sail for Philadelphia. The ship contained many Dutch immigrants to the New World. Off the coast of North America the ship was struck by a series of storms. The crew mutinied. They murdered the Captain and stole all the passengers' valuables. They then set out in lifeboats, leaving the passengers to their fate.

The ship ran aground off Block Island. The residents of the island made some income by salvaging wrecks. The wreckers took the survivors off the ship. But there was one woman who had been driven mad by the hardships. She refused to leave the wrecked *Palatine.* The wreckers set fire to the ship anyway. The blazing ship was taken out to sea with the tide. The mad woman could still be heard screaming from the burning deck.

Even today a ghostly light is sometimes seen off Block Island. According to legend the light comes from a burning ship. People call it the *"Palatine* Light."

4

THE MANY GHOSTS
OF AARON BURR

Aaron Burr was one of the most colorful characters in American history. Not one of the best—just one of the most colorful. Burr's ghost has been seen in lower Manhattan where he spent much of his life. But even more celebrated are the ghosts of some of those who were associated with Aaron Burr.

Burr was born in New Jersey in 1756. He came from a family of clergymen, but was never interested in religion. He studied law and became involved with those American colonists who wanted independence from England. When the Revolution broke out Burr joined George Washington's army. He was a brave soldier, but he could not take orders. Ill feeling

Aaron Burr

developed between Burr and Washington. In 1779, Burr resigned from the army because of poor health.

Burr then came to New York, set up a law practice, and married. He was very successful and made a lot of money. But he was always able to spend more money than he made. His mansion at Richmond Hill was the scene of some of the most brilliant (and expensive) parties in America.

Burr also entered politics. He was elected to the New York State Legislature, and later to the U.S. Senate. In the year 1800, Aaron Burr was very nearly elected President of the United States. Both Burr and Thomas Jefferson were running. The method of voting for President and Vice President was different in 1800 then it is today. The vote wound up a tie. The President was then to be chosen by the House of Representatives. The loser would become Vice President. Burr probably would have won, except for Alexander Hamilton. Hamilton was a very powerful man in the early years of this country. He did not care for Thomas Jefferson and Jefferson's ideas. But he absolutely hated Aaron Burr. Because of Hamilton's opposition, Jefferson was elected. Burr was made Vice President. Burr and Jefferson never got along either.

The Burr-Hamilton duel

In 1804, when Burr's term as Vice President was over, he knew he could not return to Washington. Jefferson was in firm control there. Burr tried to become Governor of New York. Once again Hamilton stopped him.

That campaign was unusually bitter. Burr felt he had been insulted. He demanded an apology from Hamilton. Hamilton refused, and the two agreed to fight a duel. Dueling was not legal, but it went on anyway. On July 11, 1804, the two men crossed the river from New York to Weehawken, New Jersey. Both men had fought duels before. Hamilton fired first and missed. Burr did not miss. Hamilton was taken back to New York, where he died within a few days. Burr had to flee because warrants were out for his arrest. Hamilton had many powerful friends who would try to avenge his death.

Alexander Hamilton is the first of the ghosts associated with Aaron Burr. When Hamilton was brought back from the duel he was taken first to the house of John Francis, his doctor. The house is at 27 Jane Street in Greenwich Village. Hamilton was treated there, then taken to his own home a short distance away. It was there he died.

The Hamilton house is long gone. But 27 Jane Street still exists. And some of the people who have lived there claim it is haunted by the ghost of Alexander Hamilton. No one actually reported seeing the ghost. But the house was always troubled by strange noises. It sounded as though someone were walking up and down the stairs. There was also the mysterious sound of doors opening and closing.

No one knew what was going on. So a spirit medium was brought in. She went into a trance. She thought she saw "an empty coffin, people weeping, talking, milling around, and the American flag atop the coffin; in the coffin a man's hat, shoes with silver buckles, gold epaulettes . . .'' She also said the ghost associated with the house died in great pain. All of this suggests Alexander Hamilton.

Hamilton was dead. Burr was alive, but in big trouble. He could not return to his home in New York. But he could not remain quiet either. He went West. Burr got involved in a wild scheme. He was going to organize an invasion of Mexico. He also hoped that some of the Western states would join up with Mexico. He was planning to start his own Western empire. The plans were treasonable. There was also never a chance they would have worked. One of Burr's associates betrayed him to President Jefferson. Burr was arrested and put on trial for treason. But he was let off. He had only planned, but he had never actually done anything.

Burr went to Europe. There he tried to get up an army to invade Florida. But that scheme too came to nothing.

There was only one person in the world Aaron Burr really cared for. It was his beautiful daughter, Theodosia. She was always pleading with her father to return to America. Finally, in 1814, he decided to do so. Theodosia was sailing from the South where she lived to New York to meet her father. The ship which carried her was lost. Some said it was sunk by pirates. More probably it was lost in a storm off Cape Hatteras, North Carolina. In any case, the ghost of Theodosia Burr has been seen walking across the beaches of Hatteras.

Burr was heartbroken. But he never gave up. He reopened his law office in New York. For the next twenty-two years he was a successful New York lawyer. In 1833 at the age of seventy-seven he married a wealthy widow, Eliza Jumel. She was about twenty years younger than he. But she was very nearly as notorious.

Eliza Jumel had grown up in the streets of Providence, Rhode Island. She was very beautiful. She went to New York, where men flocked about her. She may have married a Frenchman named Captain de la Croix. In any event, she moved to France with him. But she got bored and returned to New York. This time she married Stephen Jumel, one of the richest men in New York.

He bought her a huge house. It was fixed up as an elegant mansion. Eliza Jumel hoped to become the toast of New York society. But very few society people would visit the Jumel Mansion. They disliked Eliza, and she grew to hate them.

Stephen Jumel went off to Paris for a long

Theodosia Burr

Eliza Jumel

time. Eliza managed his business affairs. She was very good at it. His fortune grew. Eventually, though, he returned home. But now he was an old man. In May, 1832, he had a serious accident, and died a few days later. Gossips said that Eliza helped to kill him. There is no evidence of this. Still, people said that the mansion was haunted by the ghost of the "murdered" Stephen Jumel.

Even before her husband's death Eliza had known Aaron Burr. She married him within a year of Jumel's death. It is not hard to imagine why Burr married her. She was rich and he always needed money. It is harder to guess why she married him. But even as an old man Burr was always charming, and attractive to women.

The marriage did not last. After a short time Eliza decided to divorce Burr. The divorce was granted just a few days before Burr died.

Eliza Jumel lived on until 1865. She died in her grand mansion at the age of ninety-three. For many years she had been quite mad. Very few people ever visited her. Almost immediately after her death stories about her ghost began to spread. There were strange noises, mysterious cold drafts, and sometimes a glimpse of the ghostly form of Madame Jumel herself.

The Jumel Mansion still stands. It is considered an historic site, and is preserved by the City of New York. Children in the area sometimes say that an old lady comes out on the balcony and chases them away. No old lady lives in the house now. So it must be the ghost of old Eliza Jumel.

5

THE BERKELEY SQUARE "HORROR"

London has a lot of haunted houses. But for many years the most famous haunted house was No. 50 Berkeley Square. It was so famous that visitors to London were taken to see it—from the outside. Most of the time no one would live there.

Berkeley Square was a very fashionable place. Many well-known and wealthy people have lived there. No. 50 was once the home of George Canning. He later became Prime Minister of England. But the haunting stories did not start until after Canning left.

No one seems to know when or why the stories began. No one even knows what the "Horror" that haunted the house was supposed to look like. Many different descriptions have been given.

The house seems to have had a bad reputation by about 1840. People in the neighborhood heard strange noises. The house was supposed to be empty at the time. But it sounded as if someone, or something, was dragging heavy objects around. When neighbors investigated they found nothing. Some people suspected criminals were using the house. They may have made the noises to frighten people off.

In the 1860s the house was occupied by a Mr. Myers. He was a very odd man. He lived alone and would never let a stranger enter his house. He slept most of the day. At night he wandered about the house with a candle in hand.

It was said that once he was going to be married. He had rented No. 50 Berkeley Square as the home for himself and his future bride. But the lady rejected him at the last moment. This blow snapped his mind. The stories of the haunted house may have started with the poor man's strange behavior.

Another account held that the house was haunted by a little girl wearing Scottish kilts. She was said to have died in an upper room of the house. Another story tells of a girl named

Adeline or Adela. She was supposed to have jumped from a window on the upper floor.

Then there is the tale of Mr. Du Pré. He lived in the house about 200 years ago. He was supposed to have kept his insane brother locked in a room on the top floor. The madman was so violent no one could go near him. He had to be fed through a slot in the door. According to some stories the Berkeley Square "Horror" is the ghost of a man with horrible features. This could be Mr. Du Pré's mad brother.

Still other accounts say that the "Horror" is not human looking. It has been described as something slimy with many legs or tentacles. According to one theory, the "Horror" is not really a ghost at all. It is some unknown creature that lives in the sewers under Berkeley Square. The thing emerges from time to time at No. 50.

But if it comes out of the sewers it has to find its way to the top floor of No. 50. In fact, it has to find its way to a particular room on the top floor. That is the haunted room. A person could live safely enough in the rest of the house. But, according to legend, anyone who spent a night in the haunted room would either die or go mad.

One rumor claimed that the house had once been owned by an unknown man. It was cared for by an elderly couple. The haunted room was always kept locked and the old couple did not have a key. Every six months the unknown owner would appear. He would lock the old couple in the basement. Then he alone would enter the haunted room. He would stay in there for hours. What he did no one knew. Then he would relock the room, release the old couple, and disappear for another six months.

One person who was said to have spent a night in the haunted room was Lord Lyttleton. He knew a great deal about ghosts. His family had the reputation of being the most haunted family in England. Still, he took two loaded guns with him for protection.

The next morning he reported something jumped at him in the middle of the night. He fired a gun at it and heard it fall. But whatever it was vanished. Lord Lyttleton either could not or would not describe what had been in the room with him.

Sir Robert Warboys was not so lucky. He was said to be the first man to challenge the "Horror." He did not believe in ghosts or slimy creatures creeping up out of sewers. He thought the whole "Horror" business was sim-

The haunted house at 50 Berkeley Square

ply nonsense. He bet the owner of the house that he could spend the night in the haunted room. The owner agreed, but on one condition. A group of men would stay downstairs all night. If Sir Robert was in danger he would ring a bell twice. The men would then rush up and save him.

In the middle of the night Sir Robert's bell rang out frantically. The men ran to the stairs. Then they heard a shot. When they opened the door to the haunted room Sir Robert was already dead. His face was frozen in a look of terror. He had died of fright. The pistol was in his hand. Whatever it was that he had fired at had gotten away.

After that the house remained unoccupied for a long time. In 1887, two sailors stumbled upon it. They did not know its evil reputation. They had no money. Now it was getting dark and cold. They had no place to sleep. The empty house looked like a perfect refuge for the night.

Most of the house was unfurnished. The only room which contained furniture was the haunted room. No one had dared take anything out of it. That is where the sailors decided to sleep.

In the middle of the night they heard noises. Something was crawling or creeping toward the door of the room. The candles went out. The men never did get a good look at the thing. One of the sailors tried to attack the "Horror" with a curtain rod. The other ran out the door. He found a policeman down the street. He dragged the policeman back to No. 50. The policeman said, "You haven't been in there!"

At the foot of the stairs inside they found the other sailor. He was dead. His face, too, was frozen in an expression of terror. He had died of fright.

Even the walls of the house were said to be "saturated with electric horror." People in the neighboring house would not sit with their backs to the wall that the two buildings shared. If they did, they began to feel cold. They also got the impression that something evil was looking over their shoulders.

The Berkeley Square "Horror" has not been heard of for a long time. For over forty years No. 50 Berkeley Square has been a bookstore. The owners of the store have never been troubled by horrors. The haunted room is the accounting department. During World War II members of the staff slept in the room. They were not disturbed by anything supernatural. Tourists still visit No. 50. But the present owners have no new ghost stories to tell them.

6

DRURY LANE GHOSTS

Most people are afraid of ghosts. It is considered bad luck even to see a ghost. The rumor that a house is haunted will make it hard to rent or sell. People have tried to rid ghosts from their homes by exorcism. But there is at least one ghost who is considered a symbol of good luck. An offer to exorcise this spirit was turned down flat.

This popular ghost is the "Man in Grey of Drury Lane." Drury Lane is a famous and very old theatre in London. It has several ghosts. But the Man in Grey is far and away the best known.

The Man in Grey is a very dignified ghost. He is a handsome young man dressed in eighteenth-century clothes. His hair is powdered or he wears a wig. He wears or carries a three-cornered hat. He gets his name from his long grey cloak. The hilt of a sword has been seen sticking out from under the cloak.

The Man in Grey never moans or shrieks. He doesn't rattle chains. He doesn't even appear at night. He has been seen only between the hours of 9 A.M. and 6 P.M. He walks slowly from one end of the balcony, and disappears into the wall on the other side. He also fades away if you get too close to him. This particular ghost has only been reported backstage once. He is part of the audience, not a performer.

The Drury Lane Theatre

The Man in Grey has been seen by many people for over a century. Usually he appears during rehearsals when the theatre is almost empty. But he has also been seen during afternoon performances when the theatre is full. But not everybody can see this ghost. King George VI went to Drury Lane to see the Man in Grey. The ghost did not appear on royal command. Sometimes one or two people in a group will see him, but the others will not. It takes a special talent to see this ghost. Often people who see the Man in Grey have never heard the legend. They think he is one of the actors in costume.

No one knows who the ghost is supposed to be. But there is a story which may explain the origin of the Man in Grey. A little over a century ago workmen broke through an old wall in the upper balcony. It contained a small chamber. Inside the chamber was a skeleton with a dagger in its ribs. There were a few bits of cloth clinging to the bones. The skeleton was buried in a graveyard near the theatre. Its identity was never discovered. But the cloth remains indicated that the person had lived in the eighteenth century.

W. J. Macqueen-Pope, who was an expert on theatre history, had a theory about the skel-

Inside the Drury Lane Theatre

eton. He thought it was the remains of a young man who had been murdered. Perhaps the murderer worked for the theatre. The body was walled-up. It was not discovered until the crime had been forgotten.

But the Man in Grey is not seeking revenge, as ghosts are supposed to do. In fact, theatre people regard him as a symbol of good luck. He is often seen before a play which turns out to be a hit. Failures do not attract him. He was seen before the opening of the musicals *Oklahoma, Carousel, South Pacific* and *The King and I*. All of these shows were tremendous successes at Drury Lane.

In the 1950s there was an offer made to exorcise the Man in Grey. The people of Drury Lane rejected the idea angrily. They wished to keep their lucky ghost.

The Man in Grey is only one of the old theatre's ghosts. Drury Lane was opened during the reign of King Charles II in the seventeenth century. The king and a crowd of his attendants were seen on the theatre stage in the summer of 1948—obviously ghosts. That was during the run of *Oklahoma*. In life, King Charles had always loved the theatre.

Oklahoma was a much-haunted show at Drury Lane. Besides the Man in Grey and King Charles, there was also a ghost who was felt but not seen. A young American actress named Betty Jo Jones had a comic part in the show. Her performance was not going well. People were not laughing as much as they should.

Then during one scene she felt someone gently push her into a different position. She looked around but could see no one. The unseen hands continued to guide her around the stage. Amazingly, her performance got better. The next night the ghostly hands pushed her

The lobby of the Drury Lane

about again. Once again her performance improved. The hands gave her a friendly pat on the back.

Almost the same thing happened during *The King and I*. A young actress named Doreen Duke was trying out for a part. She was very anxious to do well. But she was also very scared. When she got on stage she felt the hands guiding her around. When she became nervous she got the same friendly pat on the back. She got the part. The hands aided her during rehearsal and on opening night.

Macqueen-Pope thought the unseen ghost may be Joe Grimaldi. He was a celebrated comic actor and singer. He had often performed at Drury Lane, and had given his farewell performance there. He was known as a good man, always willing to help fellow performers. Perhaps he kept helping them, even after death.

A tall, thin, ugly ghost has been seen backstage from time to time. It is thought to be the ghost of the actor Charles Macklin. Macklin was very short-tempered. In 1735, he had an argument with Thomas Hallam, another actor. During the argument Macklin poked at Hallam with a stick. The stick pierced Hallam's eye, and he died as a result. Macklin was charged with manslaughter, but never punished. He lived to the amazing age of 107. The tall ghost was only seen after his death. Perhaps he was doomed to haunt the scene of his unpunished crime.

A comedian named Stanley Lupino also saw a ghost at Drury Lane. He was putting on his makeup. When he looked in the mirror he saw another face reflected next to his own. It was the face of Dan Leno, another comedian who had died not long before. Later, Lupino learned he was using the dead man's favorite dressing room.

Macqueen-Pope got a letter from a woman saying she too had seen a ghost at Drury Lane. She was sitting in the theatre with her sister. At the end of the row they saw a man wearing old-fashioned clothes. The man seemed to be watching the play intently. When the lights went on he was gone. To leave the theatre he would have had to pass directly by the two women. But he had not. He had simply vanished. Later, when looking through a book of old theatre pictures, they recognized the man. It was Charles Kean, a famous actor of the nineteenth century.

Drury Lane has many ghosts. But the old theatre has also been unusually fortunate in its choice of haunts.

7

NEW ORLEANS GHOSTS

New Orleans may be the most haunted city in America. If it isn't number one, it's close.

Of all the ghosts of New Orleans the most exotic is Marie Laveau. In fact, some people are not sure that Marie Laveau is a ghost, though she was born nearly 200 years ago. The reason is that people are not sure Marie Laveau could die.

Marie Laveau was known as the voodoo queen of New Orleans. Voodoo is a collection of religious and magical practices. Many of them came from Africa. Voodoo developed among black slaves. It was particularly strong on the island of Haiti. It is still practiced there

A courtyard in New Orleans

today. Voodoo was also practiced by the slaves in New Orleans. Like Haiti, New Orleans had once been controlled by the French.

Officially, the practice of voodoo was forbidden to the slaves. But it went on anyway. Even the white masters were said to fear the power of voodoo. They often asked aid of those who were skilled in the practice. The most skilled of all was the legendary Marie Laveau.

Who she was, and where she came from, no one seems to know. There are reports that she led voodoo dances in Congo Square as early as 1830.

Many people, black and white, came to her house on St. Ann Street. They wanted magic charms and potions. She had charms and potions for everything. Some could cure disease, others could cause it. She had love potions which would attract people, and poisons to get rid of them. She could even control the weather.

At one time two Frenchmen were sentenced to be hanged. Their friends came to Marie and asked for help. Marie vowed they would not hang as scheduled. On execution day the two men were brought to the gallows in the public square. The day had been bright and sunny. But as the nooses were slipped around their necks a violent thunderstorm broke. Lightning

The French Quarter in New Orleans

flashed and thunder roared. Those who had gathered to see the execution screamed and fled. The executioner managed to open the trap door. But the wet nooses slipped off the Frenchmen's necks. They landed unhurt, on the ground below.

In the end it didn't work out all that well for the Frenchmen. They were executed at a later date. But Marie had kept her word—sort of. And it did help to build her reputation. Besides, there were no more public executions in New Orleans.

There are reliable reports that Marie was still holding voodoo ceremonies in the 1890s.

That was fifty years after she first came to notice. She wasn't supposed to look any older in 1890 either.

Some think that Marie was killed in a hurricane in the 1890s. Others are not so sure that she ever died. There are reports that after the hurricane she was seen floating on a log singing voodoo songs.

Most historians believe that there were really two Marie Laveaus. The first *original* Marie died around 1881. The death was reported in New Orleans newspapers. Her place was taken by another woman who may have been her daughter. This second Marie Laveau continued the family tradition for another ten years or so. Then she too died, or gave up voodoo and disappeared.

That is what the historians think. Other people said that there was only one Marie Laveau and that she changed herself into a big black crow. The crow can sometimes be seen flapping around the old St. Louis cemetery. Others say her spirit has been changed into a large dog or a snake.

At the St. Louis cemetery there are two unmarked tombs. Even today people occasionally leave voodoo offerings on these tombs. Some believe them to be the tomb, or tombs, of Marie Laveau.

Marie has appeared as a more traditional ghost as well. Her form has been seen many times in the vicinity of the cemetery. One person claims that the ghost of Marie Laveau hit him across the face when he failed to recognize her.

The site of Marie's old home at 1020 St. Ann Street is also rumored to be haunted by the ghosts of Marie and her followers. They are still performing their wild rituals from the spirit world.

An even more sinister New Orleans figure was Delphine Lalaurie. She was a beautiful and wealthy woman of high social position. She was also a cruel monster. She kept some of her slaves chained in the attic at her house at 1140 Royal Street. She would often torture and kill them. Today ghostly moans are often heard coming from the attic of the house. One of Delphine Lalaurie's victims was said to have slipped out of her chains and leaped to her death in the courtyard. Her dying screams still startle tourists walking down Royal Street.

A fine old house at 1113 Charles Street is supposed to be haunted by a whole army of ghosts. It was once the home of General Pierre Gustave Toutant de Beauregard. General

New Orleans during the Civil War

Beauregard was in command of the Southern forces that fired on Fort Sumter. That was the opening battle in the Civil War. He was also Southern commander at Bull Run, the first major battle of the war. Both of these engagements were successes for the South.

Beauregard took over command at the Battle of Shiloh. That was not a Southern success. In fact, the battle was a disaster for both sides. Huge numbers of men died. On balance, the Southern side was the bigger loser. They could not afford such heavy casualties. No one had expected such a bloody outcome. Later, Beauregard was heavily criticized for his leadership in that battle.

According to legend, a huge ghostly Confederate army can sometimes be seen inside the old Beauregard house. At first, they appear fit and ready for battle. A short time later, they are only a tattered and broken remnant. It is the Battle of Shiloh all over again.

A final New Orleans ghost concerns, of all things, the brother of a Turkish Sultan. This Oriental nobleman, several of his wives, and servants were supposed to have lived briefly in the Gardette-LePretre house. Locally, it is known as "The Sultan's House" or "the haunted house."

One night during a storm enemies of the Sultan's brother broke into the house. They murdered everyone inside. The murderers buried the Sultan's brother under an inscription which read: "The justice of heaven is satisfied, and the date tree shall grow on the traitor's tomb." There was a date tree growing near the house. It was called "the Death Tree." It was supposed to be bad luck even to sit under that tree.

There are also tales of ghosts being seen in the house, or of strange Oriental music coming from it.

Today the house is still around. It is divided up into expensive apartments. None of the residents are troubled by ghosts. But old-times in the area will still speak of "the haunted house."

8

SCREAMING SKULLS

There are several screaming skulls in England. These are real skulls. They have the reputation of making loud noises, or becoming troublesome in other ways, if they are moved.

The best known of these is the screaming skull of Bettiscombe Manor. Bettiscombe Manor is a large farmhouse in the county of Dorset. The skull is usually kept in a cardboard box stored in a bureau drawer.

According to local legend the skull is that of a black slave. The slave was brought to Bettiscombe in the eighteenth century. He was promised that on his death his body would be returned to Africa for burial. The slave told his

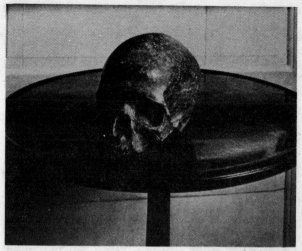

The screaming skull of Bettiscombe Manor

master that if the promise was not carried out a curse would fall on Bettiscombe Manor.

When the slave did die, the promise was forgotten. His body was buried in a local churchyard, not far from the house. Almost at once people began hearing roars and screams from the tomb. The local people began to object. They wanted to get the restless corpse out of their graveyard. Finally, the owner of Bettiscombe Manor had the body dug up. It was taken to the house and stored in a loft. Over the years only the skull remained. No one is exactly sure why. In one version of the legend the body was shipped to Africa (or the West

Indies). For some reason the skull was kept in England.

There are many stories of what took place when someone tried to remove the skull. Once it was thrown in a pond. That night the house was so troubled by screams and noises that the skull had to be fished out. When it was returned to the house all was quiet again.

Another time the skull was buried in a hole nine feet deep. Within three days the skull had burrowed to the surface. The owner of the house found it waiting to be taken back inside.

Other ghostly tales are also attached to the skull. According to one, on a particular night of the year a phantom coach goes from Bettiscombe Manor, along a lonely road, to the churchyard. Local people call it "the funeral procession of the skull."

In the 1960s the writer Eric Marple spent a night in the house with the skull. He didn't hear any screaming. But he was badly troubled by nightmares. He refused to stay another night. The owners of the house weren't bothered by the skull. Of course, they didn't try to take it outside either.

Many think of the skull as sort of a good-luck charm. It is supposed to protect the house from ghosts and evil spirits.

In a slightly different version of the legend

the slave and his master had a fight to the death. The skull belongs to one of them. But no one knows which one. To add to the puzzle, scientists who have examined the skull say it really belongs to a woman. And a prehistoric woman at that. Where did it come from? How did the story about the slave start? No one today can answer those questions.

The screaming skull kept at Wardley Hall near Manchester has an even more romantic reputation. It is supposed to have belonged to Roger Downes who lived in the seventeenth century. The Downes family owned Wardly Hall then. Roger was a violent man. He had killed at least one other person. Roger himself was killed during a fight on London Bridge. He was beheaded by one of the watchmen. His head was then sent to his sister who lived at Wardly Hall.

Every time the skull has been removed from Wardly Hall it has mysteriously returned. It is always kept on a little shelf under the stairs. Once it was just moved from its usual place. That night there was a violent storm. Wardly Hall was badly damaged. Since then the owners of the house have decided it is best to leave the skull alone.

As usual with such legends there is great

confusion. Someone opened Roger Downes' tomb about a hundred years ago. It contained a full skeleton. Well, almost full. Only the top of the skull was missing. Just why, no one seems to know. But that means that the skull at Wardly Hall does not belong to Roger Downes.

Whose is it? The most likely candidate is Ambrose Barlow. Barlow was a monk. In the seventeenth century when Barlow lived, there was a lot of anti-religious hysteria in England. Many priests and monks were executed. Barlow was one of them. His head was cut off and put on display.

But the owner of Wardly Hall sympathized with the unfortunate Barlow. He took the monk's head and hid it in his house. Years passed. The owner of Wardly Hall died. Everyone forgot about the skull of the monk. Then one day a servant ran across it by accident. Seeing no use for an old skull, he tossed it into the moat. That night there was a violent storm. The next morning the owners of Wardly Hall had the moat drained. They found the skull, and so the legend of the screaming skull of Wardly Hall began.

There is another screaming skull in a farmhouse in Derbyshire. According to tradition,

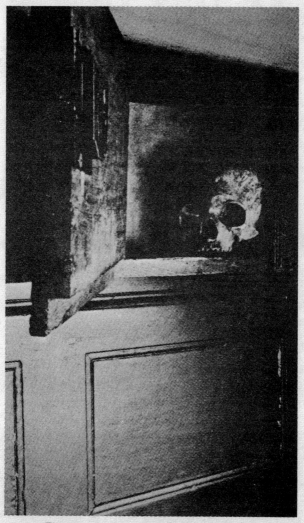

The screaming skull of Wardly Hall

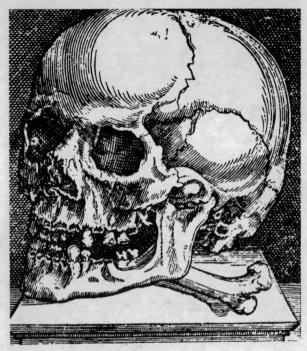

Do skulls really scream?

the skull belonged to a young woman. She had been murdered in the house centuries ago. Before she died she placed a curse on the house. She said that terrible things would happen if her remains were ever moved from the spot at which she died.

But for some reason the local people called the skull by a man's name—Dickie.

Dickie is not a very frightening name. The

skull does not have a very frightening reputation either. Of course, if it is moved, crops are supposed to wither and cattle die. So no one moves it. Dickie is looked on more as a guardian spirit or good-luck charm.

Once a railway line was supposed to have been built in the area. The local people didn't want trains running by, waking them up and frightening their cattle. But there was nothing they could do to stop the railroad. Then the railway builders ran into all sorts of problems. They tried to build a bridge but the soil was too soft. Finally, the line was diverted to another area.

The local people were very happy. They gave Dickie all the credit. They said he didn't want noisy trains so close to his home. So he used his supernatural powers to stop them.

Dickie is a great favorite.

9

CALIFORNIA'S GHOST HOUSE

The most celebrated ghost house in America isn't exactly haunted. It was built for ghosts. It is a rambling 160-room mansion in California's Santa Clara Valley.

The builder of this strange house was Sara L. Winchester. In the mid-nineteenth century she married William Winchester. He was the son and heir of Oliver Fisher Winchester, the "rifle king." He was also a millionaire many times over.

Sara seemed to have everything. Then quite suddenly she had nothing. Within a year her husband and only child died. The double tragedy seemed to have affected her mind. She be-

Winchester rifles, the foundation of a family fortune

came deeply depressed. No one could snap her out of it.

Sara Winchester had always been interested in spiritualism. In one of her rare outings she attended a séance in Boston. The medium was Adam Coons. The medium told her that the spirit of her husband was standing beside her. Coons then told Sara that the spirit had a task for her. She was to build a house for the spirits of all those men killed by Winchester rifles. Since the Winchester was the most popular rifle in the world, the house would have to be huge.

Sara Winchester took this spirit message seriously. She sold her home in New Haven, Connecticut. Then she headed West. She believed that the spirit of her husband would guide her.

After a long cross-country journey she reached California. In the Santa Clara Valley she saw a large house being built. The spirits told her this was the place. She immediately bought the house from the owner, a California doctor.

Of course she wanted changes in the building plan. When she began to explain the changes to the builder he realized he was not dealing with a normal person. He quit the job at once. But Sara Winchester didn't have to worry. There were always plenty of others willing to work for the money she paid.

She lived for thirty-six more years. Practically all of that time she devoted to adding to, tearing down and changing her ghost house. The building went on seven days a week. There were no breaks for Sundays and holidays on this job. Sara was getting her plans directly from the spirit world. The spirits would not wait.

The final result was the largest private home in the world. It is also a mad jumble. There are stairways that lead nowhere. Elevators go up only one floor. Doors open on blank walls, or worse, to drop-offs.

The outside of the house is also a jumble.

Doors join windows. Rooms and whole wings are just stuck on. There are peaks and spires all over the top of the structure. One writer compared it to the crazy house in an amusement park.

During Sara Winchester's lifetime the house was mostly hidden from view by huge hedges and trees. A crew of gardeners was forever working to make the greenery thicker. Today only the peaks of the house can be seen from a distance.

Sara Winchester believed in the power of the number 13. It can be found everywhere in the house. Most rooms have 13 windows. Chandeliers have 13 lights. There are 13 bathrooms in the house. Most of the stairways have 13 steps, and so on. On one stairway she changed the pattern. It has fourty-four steps. But it only goes up one floor—ten feet in all.

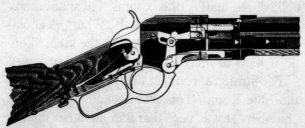

Sectional cut of a Winchester rifle, showing position after firing. Winchesters were very popular rifles.

There was sort of a mad logic to this building. Sara Winchester was trying to confuse the evil or vengeful spirits she felt might pursue her. The house could certainly confuse any living person.

Life inside the house was as strange as its appearance. Sara herself wandered about like a ghost. Every night she slept in a different bedroom. When she had run through them all, she started again.

Sara's needs were tended to by a full staff of servants. They were well paid, and did not gossip. Visitors were discouraged. It was said that President Theodore Roosevelt was turned away. So was Mary Baker Eddy, founder of Christian Science. Strangely, the magician Harry Houdini was supposed to have been invited inside the ghost house. Houdini had a deep interest in spiritualism. But he did not believe the claims of mediums. He spent many years exposing them as frauds. What the ghost-ridden old woman had to say to the great skeptic is hard to imagine.

The strangest room in this strange house was the Blue Room. This was a small, windowless chamber. It was here that Sara held her nightly séances. No one else was ever allowed to enter the room at that time. No one living, that is. Every night, at midnight, a bell would ring.

Sara, wearing a long gown decorated with strange symbols, would enter the Blue Room for her ghostly meetings.

Sometimes there were more festive occasions for the spirits of the dead. There were regular banquets in the formal dining room. The table was always set for thirteen—Sara Winchester and twelve guests that no one else could see. The ghosts were served the most expensive of food on gold plates. The servants undoubtedly took care of the uneaten meals.

In the thirty-six years she lived in the house, Sara is known to have gone to town only once. She did leave for several years after the San Francisco earthquake of 1906. When the quake hit, Sara was asleep. She thought the evil spirits had finally gotten to her house. The servants tried to rescue her, but they did not know which bedroom she was sleeping in, so it took a long time to find her. They finally located her, terrified but unhurt. She ordered that bedroom boarded up, and no one went into it ever again while she lived.

After the earthquake Sara got the idea the world was going to be destroyed by flood. She had a large houseboat built on a piece of land she owned. When it was completed she moved into it. There she lived for six years, waiting for the waters to overwhelm the land. Finally, she got tired of waiting, and moved back into the house in Santa Clara Valley.

Sara Winchester died in her ghost house in September of 1922. She was eighty-five years old. If the ghosts of the men killed by Winchester rifles finally got her, they had been very slow about it.

Today the ghost house is haunted only by tourists. For a small admission price anyone can walk where a President was once refused admittance. But the tourists stay close to their guides. They don't want to get lost in Sara Winchester's ghost house.

10

THE WEST POINT GHOST

The U.S. Military Academy at West Point is about as tradition-ridden a place as any in America. Its grim but stately buildings seem a perfect place for ghosts. And, indeed, several have been reported there.

One of the more popular ones is a maid named Molly. She haunts the Superintendent's house. Living maids make the beds. Molly goes around rumpling them up. She is not a very frightening ghost.

The most recent West Point ghost appeared late in 1972. There are several versions of this ghost story. This is the one that is best known.

The ghost was supposed to have appeared in room 4714 of the 47th Division Barracks.

The library at West Point

On the night of October 21, 1972, the room was occupied by two lowerclassmen. One of them, a nineteen-year-old cadet, was awakened by a strange sound in the middle of the night. He saw what he thought was a ghostly figure coming through the door. He woke up his roommate, but by that time the figure had vanished.

The next night the strange figure appeared

again. This time both of the cadets in the room saw it. They let out a yell. Cadet Captain Keith W. Bakken heard them and rushed to the room. He saw nothing but said that the room felt unnaturally cold. The next night the Cadet Captain himself stayed in the room. Nothing happened.

Captain Bakken then found an upperclassman to share the room with the freshmen. At about two in the morning it happened again. All three men said they saw "a figure partially extended out of the wall." It disappeared almost immediately. But the spot on the wall felt "icy cold."

All three witnesses agreed that the figure was that of a soldier in an old-fashioned uniform. He had a handlebar mustache, and carried a nineteenth-century musket.

Later, the three did some research in the West Point library. They found that uniforms worn in the 1830s were most similar to those that the ghostly figure had worn.

The incident created quite a bit of excitement at West Point. Other cadets reported having seen the figure, or something very like it, in the room. Different cadets slept in the room. Some had strange experiences; others did not.

Finally, the commanding officer of West

The West Point ghost wore a cadet uniform of the 1830s.

Point declared the whole "haunted room" off-limits. Even the furniture was removed. But cadets kept popping in for a look anyway.

The story of the ghost in Room 4714 was carried in newspapers all over the country. West Point officials don't like that sort of publicity. They were not very happy about all the attention the ghost was getting. They tried to play it down.

In November, Midshipman William Gravell of the U.S. Naval Academy at Annapolis, Maryland, said that the whole thing was a hoax. He confessed to being the hoaxer. He said the ghost had only been a picture projected on the wall. The feeling of cold was produced by carbon dioxide escaping from a fire extinguisher. The Naval Academy and West Point have always been rivals. The hoax was supposed to be a Halloween prank. The incident took place near Halloween.

That should have closed the case. But it didn't. Many people still don't believe Midshipman Gravell's "confession." They say he could not possibly have done what he said he did.

People continued to talk about what the cadets really did see in Room 4714.

A student newspaper called *The Pointer* had

The cadet barracks as shown some years ago

some guesses about whose ghost had been
seen. The building with the haunted room is
not far from the spot where an officer's house
burned down about a century ago. The officer
was killed in the fire. The building is also not
far from an old graveyard.

Whatever its origin, the ghost of West Point

has not been seen since the middle of November, 1972. Whether it will appear again no one can say. But it has definitely become part of the folklore of ghosts. As such, it is in the distinguished company of Abraham Lincoln, Anne Boleyn, Marie Laveau, Eliza Jumel, and many, many others.

INDEX

ABOUT THE AUTHOR

DANIEL COHEN is the author of many books for both young readers and adults, and he is a former managing editor of *Science Digest* magazine. His titles include *Supermonsters, The Greatest Monsters in the World, Real Ghosts, Creatures from UFO's, The World's Most Famous Ghosts, The Monsters of Star Trek, Missing! Stories of Strange Disappearances* and *Famous Curses,* all of which are available in Archway Paperback editions.

Mr. Cohen was born in Chicago and has a degree in journalism from the University of Illinois. He appears frequently on radio and television and has lectured at colleges and universities throughout the country. He lives with his wife, young daughter, two dogs and three cats in Port Jervis, New York.